The Civil War

RECONSTRUCTION: THE YEARS FOLLOWING THE CIVIL WAR

Linda R. Wade

ABDO
Daughters Publishing

Visit us at
www.abdopub.com

Published by Abdo Publishing Company, 4940 Viking Drive, Edina, MN 55435.
Copyright ©1998 by Abdo Consulting Group, Inc. International copyrights
reserved in all countries. No part of this book may be reproduced in any form
without written permission from the publisher.

Printed in the United States.

Graphic Design: John Hamilton
Contributing Editors: John Hamilton; Alan Gergen; Elizabeth Clouter-Gergen
Cover photos: John Hamilton; Digital Stock
Interior photos: Digital Stock, pages 4, 7, 8, 9, 15, 16, 18
                 Corbis, pages 5, 11, 19, 21, 22, 23, 24, 25, 26, 27
                 AP/Wide World Photos, pages 12, 14,
                 National Archives, pages 1, 17

Sources: Barnes, Eric Wollencott. *The War Between the States.* New York:
McGraw-Hill Book Co., 1959; Jordan, Robert P. *The Civil War.* Washington,
D.C.: National Geography Society, 1969; Levenson, Dorothy. *Reconstruction.*
New York: Franklin Watts, 1970; *Our Great Heritage. . . from the Beginning,
1866-1896, Vol. 7.* Chicago, 1975; Ray, Delia. *Behind the Blue and the Gray.*
New York: Lodestar Books, 1991; Reger, James P. *Life in the North During the
Civil War.* San Diego, CA: Lucent Books, 1997; Reger, James P. *Life in the South
During the Civil War.* San Diego, CA: Lucent Books, 1997; Sandler, Martin W.
Civil War. New York: Harper Collins Pub., 1996.

Library of Congress Cataloging–in–Publication Data

Wade, Linda R.
   Reconstruction: the years following the Civil War / Linda R. Wade
      p. cm. — (The Civil War)
   Includes index.
   Summary: Looks at the period known as Reconstruction which followed the
Civil War, and the passing of the fifteenth amendment to the Constitution.
   ISBN 1-56239-821-0
   1. Reconstruction—Juvenile literature. [1. Reconstruction. 2. United States—
History—1865-1898.] I. Title. II. Series: Wade, Linda R. Civil War.
E668.W26 1998
973.8—dc21   97-37104
                                               CIP
                                               AC

CONTENTS

INTRODUCTION

The Civil War ended in April 1865. During the previous four years, there had been much destruction. The South was destroyed in the path of General Sherman's march. The North was struggling, too.

Families had been torn apart. Almost every family lost someone to the war. Husbands, fathers, and sons had been killed. Women worked to keep their families together. Many of the men who survived were without an arm or leg, or they were sick.

But the war was over. The killing stopped. It was time to rebuild the nation. It was time for the United States to unite and be one country. It was time to rebuild and come together.

Above: Former slaves celebrate their freedom at the end of the Civil War.
Facing page: The ruins of the Norfolk Navy Yard, Virginia.

CHAPTER 1

WHAT WAS RECONSTRUCTION?

Long before the war was over, the president knew he needed a plan to reunite the country. Bloodshed would come to an end. In December 1863, President Abraham Lincoln revealed what his postwar reconstruction policy would be. He knew it would not be easy to pull the country together. However, he was determined to try.

Lincoln proposed a plan that he felt would be fair, and would help the country heal from the wounds of war. His plan offered a pardon to every Southerner who took an oath to support the Union. He said that when 10 percent of a state's voters took the oath, the state could form a new government and adopt a new constitution. Their constitution had to prohibit slavery. The 10 percent would be based on the number of people who had voted in the 1860 presidential election. But even before the war was over, Northerners said Lincoln's plan was too easy on the South.

Facing page: President Abraham Lincoln.

During the spring of 1865, Lincoln discussed with General Ulysses S. Grant and his generals the peace terms to be offered to the Southern forces. Again, he emphasized his desire to go easy with the former Confederates, and to restore their rights as citizens as soon as possible.

Then the good news came. The war was finally over! Word of Confederate General Lee's surrender at Appomattox Court House spread fast. As Union soldiers heard the news, they

Grant at Cold Harbor, Virginia.

threw their knapsacks and canteens into the air and "howled like mad." Soon they left for home. It was time to get on with the business of living. They wanted to see their families. It was spring and they had corn to plant. Church bells rang out in every Northern town. People clapped and cheered.

It was not so in the South. As Confederate soldiers went home, they saw the ravages of war. Many of their homes had been burned. Their fields were trampled. Their factories were burned. Roads and bridges were destroyed or ruined. Sometimes the soldiers could not find their families. Former slaves had nothing but their freedom. One said, "I have no land, no cow, no mule."

Hard times were ahead for all the people, both in the North and the South, the white and the black.

Lincoln's Reconstruction plan was badly needed. But strong opposition to his lenient policies emerged among the so-called Radical Republicans. They were intent on punishing the South for causing war and maintaining slavery. They wanted to make sure Southern slaveholders had learned a lesson. They offered no compensation to slaveholders who had lost their slaves. They were not the least bit generous to the people in the South. They changed the policies, saying that Congress should set the Reconstruction plan instead of the president.

The ruins of a train switching station in Atlanta, Georgia.

The Radical Republicans presented their own program. The Committee on Reconstruction was formed. It recommended laws to rebuild the South the way Radical Republicans wanted it rebuilt. They prohibited any former Confederate officer from holding public office. They required the former Confederate states to reapply for statehood with new constitutions. One condition for statehood was ratifying the 14th Amendment. This amendment gave blacks and all men born or naturalized in the United States all the rights of citizenship. The Radical Republicans simply said they would not vote for reinstatement of the states until they proved they were willing to treat the blacks fairly.

It was not easy for Southerners to accept this drastic change. The blacks that were formerly their slaves were now granted the right to vote. They could hold political office and serve in the local militia.

Southerners were deeply hostile toward Northerners who made laws affecting the South, especially the Radical Republicans. They called these intruders "carpetbaggers," who worked with their "scalawag" associates.

Three days before he was assassinated, Lincoln delivered an important address to a large crowd on the White House lawn. He admitted that there was no signed agreement in the North on the proper course for Southern Reconstruction. He told the crowd that he was still open to suggestions.

Facing page: An illustration showing a carpetbagger, helped by the military, as a heavy burden to the South.

CHAPTER 2

THE ASSASSINATION OF PRESIDENT LINCOLN

The Civil War took its toll on President Lincoln. He looked sad. His eyes seemed to droop. He appeared to be very tired. He needed to relax and have an enjoyable evening.

Playing at Ford's Theatre in Washington, D.C., was a group performing a play called *Our American Cousin*. It was Good Friday, and President and Mrs. Lincoln decided to attend the evening performance. He knew it was dangerous to appear in public. Since his election in 1860, he had received a series of threats on his life. It was easier to kill a president in 1865 because very little protection was provided.

John Wilkes Booth was an actor who could not accept the fact that the South had lost the war. He devised a plan to kill the president. Others were to kill Vice President Johnson and General Ulysses S. Grant, as well as various cabinet officials.

Facing page: John Wilkes Booth leaps to the stage of Ford's Theatre after shooting President Lincoln.

John Wilkes Booth.

On the morning of April 14, 1865, Booth stopped by Ford's Theatre and found out that both Lincoln and Grant were planning to attend a special performance that evening. Immediately, Booth put his plan into action. He contacted those who were part of the scheme. They met in a nearby bar and drank whiskey. Then Booth headed for the theater.

That afternoon General and Mrs. Grant sent a message saying they would not be attending the theater. They were going to Philadelphia instead. However, Lincoln and his wife were looking forward to an enjoyable evening.

They arrived at the theater about 8:30 p.m. The audience cheered as the president and his party were seated in the flag-draped box overlooking the stage. A White House guard assigned to protect Lincoln took a seat from which he could also see the play.

Seated in a rocking chair, Lincoln was thoroughly enjoying the play. No one noticed Booth as he walked toward the door of the president's box.

He waited until loud laughter rang out. Then he opened the door and fired a pistol at the president. He ran to the edge of the box and jumped down onto the stage. He broke his left leg, but managed to hobble away.

For a long moment the audience was silent. Then Mrs. Lincoln screamed. Her husband had been shot. The bullet entered his brain and lodged behind his eye. A physician from the audience said the president would not survive.

President Lincoln was carried to a nearby boarding house. During the night, friends came to see him. They sympathized with Mrs. Lincoln. Robert, Lincoln's son, stayed at the bedside of his father. At 7:22 a.m., on April 15, 1865, Abraham Lincoln died. He was 54 years old. Secretary of War Edwin Stanton said, "Now he belongs to the ages."

The exterior of Ford's Theatre (center) in Lincoln's time.

Lincoln's flag-draped box overlooking the stage.

Telegraph wires rapidly carried the news all over the country. Sounds of victory were drowned in sorrow. A train carried the body of the president to his home in Springfield, Illinois. It stopped at cities along the route so people could pay tribute to the man they admired. Mourners lined the railroad tracks. Even in driving rains, men, women, and children stood and waited for the train to pass. Twelve days after leaving Washington, D.C., the funeral party reached Springfield.

Grieving citizens walked by their martyred president's body. On May 4, he was laid to rest in Oak Ridge Cemetery in Springfield, Illinois. His son, Willie, who had died in 1862, was buried next to him.

John Wilkes Booth did not escape. On April 26, he was tracked to a barn near Bowling Green, Virginia. The barn caught fire, and Booth was fatally shot. Others whom he had plotted with to attack various government officials were caught and hanged.

Both Northerners and Southerners mourned Lincoln's death. Although Lincoln represented the victorious enemy, his compassion and willingness to welcome the South back into the Union led Southerners to trust him. Flags were flown at half-mast for a month.

The four persons condemned as "conspirators" in Lincoln's assassination are executed by hanging.

CHAPTER 3

THE HEALING BEGINS

Andrew Johnson was the new president of the United States. He knew there was much to do before the country could heal and come together. He had worked with President Lincoln and helped to devise the plan of Reconstruction. But first, it was time to celebrate victory. The war was indeed over. Men were finally home.

On May 23, the flag of the United States flew at full staff above the White House for the first time since Lincoln's death. This was the

The Union army parades down Pennsylvania Avenue.

President Andrew Johnson.

beginning of a three-day parade. Union armies of the East and West began marching in a grand review down Pennsylvania Avenue in Washington, D.C. The next day, General Sherman led his army along the same route. People cheered loudest as his troops marched by. It was the most magnificent parade the capital had ever seen. America's bloodiest war was over, and the people wanted to celebrate.

CHAPTER 4

FIRST STEPS FOR RECONSTRUCTION

President Lincoln had already faced the question of how to treat the Southern states that had seceded from the Union. He had a plan to deal with the Southerners who had supported the Confederacy. President Johnson wanted to follow Lincoln's proposed plan. Lincoln wanted to accomplish reunification before Congress could meet and get involved. But he did not live to finish the job.

With Lincoln gone, President Johnson did not seem certain how to proceed. He tried to continue with the plan as he understood it. The Lincoln-Johnson plan did not favor a severe punishment of the South. The plan said that the South had suffered enough already. The South needed mercy, not vengeance. However, hope for a generous and peaceful reconciliation with the South died with President Lincoln.

The status of black people soon became the most crucial issue of Reconstruction. It became evident that the South, though unable to enslave the blacks, was intent upon disregarding their rights. Black people were still intimidated and beaten. Segregation was introduced. Before the war, black people were simply slaves. Equality was not an issue. After the war, blacks were given freedom and were to be treated the same as white people. For many Southerners, this was difficult.

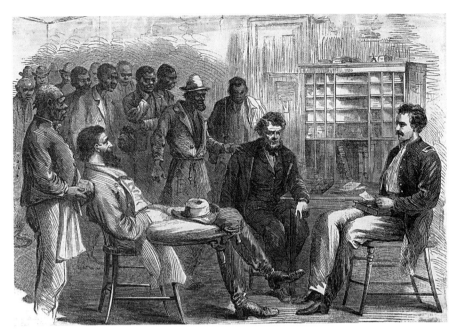

An engraving showing a group of African Americans lined up at the Freedmen's Bureau in Memphis, Tennessee.

The 13th Amendment was proposed on January 31, and ratified on December 6, 1865. It made the Emancipation Proclamation law by prohibiting slavery in the United States. The 14th Amendment came about the next year. It guaranteed United States citizenship to blacks.

On March 3, 1865, Congress established the Freedmen's Bureau to assist newly freed blacks. The bureau was staffed mainly by men from the army. They furnished food, clothing, and medical services. They supervised labor contracts between black people and their employers. The bureau also assumed the task of guiding and protecting blacks within the South. One of the most important goals of the bureau was to set up schools for black children. Teachers from the North quickly moved south to teach the basics of reading, writing, and math.

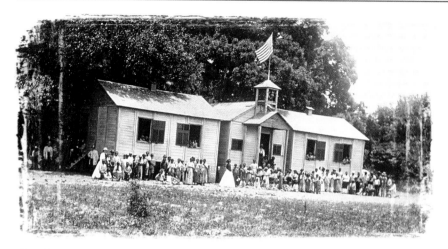

Students and teachers pose outside the Freedmen's Bureau school in Beaufort, South Carolina.

Many Southerners saw the bureau as yet another outside interference. However, the main purpose of the Freedmen's Bureau was to provide educational opportunities for blacks, and to teach them how to farm and become self-sufficient. Many black people already had this knowledge, but they were given encouragement and help during this difficult time.

President Johnson's plan called for a series of laws, which were called the Black Codes. These were state laws made in 1865-66 that regulated the activities of blacks in the South. Each state had its own set of codes. Not all were good. One forced blacks to sign contracts stating that they must remain on the same job for a year. Another said that employers could whip their workers. Some states said that blacks could not own land or carry guns.

Portrait of African American schoolchildren in New Bern, North Carolina.

Early in 1867, Congress passed a series of laws called the

Reconstruction Acts. Military districts were formed. A plan outlined the process of readmission for the 10 Southern states that had not rejoined the Union. A program of black voter registration was set up. Election boards were to register all adult black males. With the ratification of the 14th Amendment, states could apply for statehood.

The military districts caused a great deal of hardship on the people. The South was organized into 10 Southern states with 5 military districts. Each district was to be commanded by a general. Military rule prevailed to protect the Freedmen. However, many people thought that this military occupation on the South created worse conditions than had existed during the war itself. In time, these states could regain their Constitutional power and end the military rule. However, they had to meet certain conditions. They had to hold Constitutional conventions, ratify the 14th Amendment, and guarantee Freedmen the right to vote.

A log cabin built by former slaves in Oklahoma Territory. This was Native American territory where African Americans escaping slavery were welcomed.

During the 12 years of Reconstruction, the military governors who controlled the Southern states did away with the Black Codes.

Congressmen from the North were still afraid that slavery would once again be promoted. They knew it was hard for the Southern farmers to do all the work. In fact, many Southerners did refuse the new regulations. In places where plantations still existed, wealthy Southern families tried to live the same kind of lifestyle they had before the war. But this was impossible. They did not have the slaves to do the work. Without workers, the fields went unplanted.

At the same time, many freed slaves were hungry and homeless. They had no money, education or job training. They ended up with little choice but to go to work for their former masters as sharecroppers. A sharecropper worked the land owned by another and gave a portion of his crops to the landlord as rent. Often the landlords were unfair in their payment.

Two young boys from a sharecropper family picking crops in a bean field.

An illustration showing Freedmen voting in New Orleans, after being herded to the polls by carpetbaggers.

Voting was still difficult for blacks because they could not read or write. They could not afford to pay the poll tax required to vote. There was still racial injustice and a great deal of prejudice.

Another reason that voting was difficult was the Ku Klux Klan. This was a terrorist organization that spread rapidly within the South. Its members put on white robes and spent many nights galloping over the countryside to visit "offensive" blacks and whites. They frightened them with their ghostly appearance. In other instances they used violence, especially whippings, to get their messages across. They wanted to keep blacks from voting. The federal government stepped in with a series of measures to protect black voters. However, the Klan's terror tactics were often successful.

Two members of the Ku Klux Klan.

CHAPTER 5

IMPEACHMENT

The Radical Republicans had created problems for President Lincoln. With the death of Lincoln, they thought that President Johnson might be more willing to support their program for Southern Reconstruction. However, they found that Johnson was lenient toward the Southern upper-class leaders.

There was another reason why the Radicals created problems for Johnson. He was a Democrat, and the Republicans were afraid they would be voted out and lose their congressional seats. Johnson also vetoed proposals expanding the Freedmen's Bureau and a Civil Rights bill designed to protect black voting and legal rights. Then he violated the Tenure of Office Act of 1867. This act said he could not remove any official whose appointment originally required Senate approval. President Johnson called this an infringement on the traditional balance of powers and vetoed it. However, Congress overrode his veto.

Five months later, in August 1867, Johnson became upset with his secretary of war, Edwin Stanton. Stanton was a

Edwin Stanton.

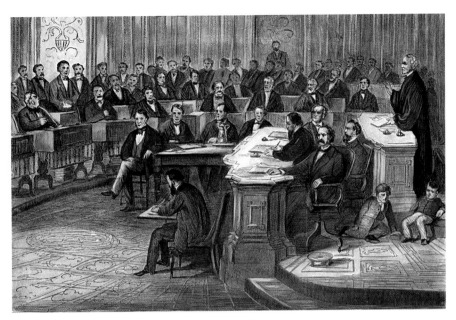

An engraving showing a courtroom scene during the impeachment of President Andrew Johnson.

Radical Republican. He had been actively working against the president's policies. So Johnson asked for Stanton's resignation.

In January, Johnson reinstated Stanton to office. However, he dismissed him again in February. The Radicals attacked the president and attempted to impeach and remove him from office.

A resolution to impeach the president was passed by the House of Representatives on February 24, 1868. No specific grounds for this action were given. A committee was appointed to develop the case against Johnson. Eleven charges were presented, eight of them dealing with his removal of Stanton. The trial began on March 5. There was not enough evidence of presidential wrongdoing to find him guilty. In the end, the president escaped conviction by one vote. The trial ended just as a presidential campaign got underway. The nation was able to put this crisis behind it. A new president, Ulysses S. Grant, the former general of the U.S. Army, easily won the election. He promised to bring the country together.

CHAPTER 6

THE EFFECTS OF RECONSTRUCTION

Some good things came about as a result of the Reconstruction period. The South began to rebuild. The public school system gave learning opportunities to black children as well as white children.

However, Reconstruction failed to solve other problems. Black people still found it difficult to buy land. Older blacks were unable to read and write. They found it easier to work for the same people they had served as slaves. Still, at least on paper, they had their freedom. They were able to set up churches. They could come and go as they wished. However, they stayed away from the whites. In fact, there was no racial harmony. The division of black and white became more intense.

Reconstruction created a deep-seated Southern hatred of the North and of the Republican Party. The South became a Democratic stronghold. Southerners wanted nothing to do with the Yankees of the North. In their hearts, they were still Confederate rebels.

Probably the best things to come out of the Reconstruction years were the 13th, 14th, and 15th Constitutional Amendments. These amendments gave equality, at least on paper, and provided the legal basis of the civil rights movement in years to come.

All federal troops were withdrawn from the South by 1877. The North and South had begun to work together. Reconstruction was at an end. The United States became one. The Civil War was finally over.

INTERNET SITES

Civil War Forum
AOL keyword: Civil War

This comprehensive site on America Online is a great place to start learning more about the Civil War. The forum is divided into four main groups. In the "Mason-Dixon Line Chat Room" you can interact with fellow Civil War buffs. The "Civil War Information Center" is especially good for historians and reenactors, and includes help with tracking down your Civil War ancestors. The "Civil War Archive" is full of downloadable text and graphic files, including old photos from the National Archives. When you're ready for more in-depth information, the "Civil War Internet" group provides many links to other sites.

The United States Civil War Center
http://www.cwc.lsu.edu/civlink.htm

This is a very extensive index of Civil War information available on the Internet, including archives and special collections, biographies, famous battlefields, books and films, maps, newspapers, and just about everything you would want to find on the Civil War. The site currently has over 1,800 web links.

These sites are subject to change. Go to your favorite search engine and type in "Civil War" for more sites.

PASS IT ON

Civil War buffs: educate readers around the country by passing on interesting information you've learned about the Civil War. Maybe your family visited a famous Civil War battle site, or you've taken part in a reenactment. Who's your favorite historical figure from the Civil War? We want to hear from you!

To get posted on the ABDO & Daughters website, E-mail us at "History@abdopub.com"

Visit the ABDO & Daughters website at www.abdopub.com

GLOSSARY

Carpetbaggers

Northerners who went to the South to take advantage of business opportunities.

Committee on Reconstruction

The committee of Radical Republicans who set up plans to rebuild the South.

14th Amendment

Constitutional amendment giving black people the right to citizenship.

Freedmen's Bureau

An organization set up to protect the interests of African Americans.

Ku Klux Klan

A secret society organized in the South after the Civil War to reassert white supremacy using terroristic methods.

Poll Tax

A tax levied on people in a community, rather than property, often as a requirement for voting.

Radical Republicans

Group of Northern congressmen who felt the government should take strong action to protect the rights of African Americans. The Radical Republicans wanted to punish the people of the South for causing the war and maintaining slavery.

Rebels

Confederate soldiers. Also a term often used to refer to all Southerners.

Reconstruction Acts

Congressional plan designed to readmit Southern states back into the Union.

Scalawags

Southerners who worked with the Radical Republicans to control politics.

Segregation

Separation of groups of people, and often used to describe differences in race.

Sharecropper

A person who works the land owned by someone else and receives a share of the profit.

Tenure of Office Act

Congressional act prohibiting the president from removing any official whose appointment required Senate approval.

13th Amendment

Prohibited slavery in the United States.

Yankees

Union soldiers. Also often used to refer to all Northerners.

Martyr

A person who dies for a cause.

Mourner

A person who is sad and grieving about the death of someone well loved.

Reunification

To come back together as one.

Telegraph

A system for communicating. A message was sent by a dash and dot code over high wires.

INDEX